IN MY OWN WORDS

1

INTENTACT®
Intentions to Actions Leadership
Leadership | Mindfulness | Development
www.intentact.com

Copyright© 2023

Author: Pam Marcheski
Designed by: Shane Breeze

WELCOME

This book is a collection of personal insights, reflections, and mantras that have been carefully curated and refined over years of introspection and experience. This book is a celebration of the wisdom gained through life's journeys, and the power of words to inspire and transform us.

Through a combination of personal anecdotes and inspiring quotes, this book offers a glimpse into the author's journey of self-discovery and personal growth. Each page is thoughtfully designed, featuring vibrant photography that enhances the message and creates a visual experience that engages the reader.

The pages are filled with insights on love, loss, gratitude, and resilience, along with practical advice on how to cultivate a life of purpose and fulfillment. This book is a reminder that even in the most challenging moments, there is always something to be learned, something to be gained, and something to be celebrated.

Whether you're looking for inspiration, guidance, or simply a beautiful book to enjoy, this collection of quotes and mantras is sure to leave a lasting impact.

EVERYTHING BEGINS WITH AWARENESS...

*"NOTICING IS THE GIFT, SPACE IS THE GRACE,
RESPONSE IS THE POWER."*

When we cultivate awareness and give ourselves space to process our experiences, we can increase our ability to respond in a way that is beneficial for ourselves and those around us.

The first part of the phrase, "noticing is the gift," reminds us of the importance of being present and aware in our lives. By noticing our thoughts, emotions, and reactions without judgment, we can gain insight.

The second part of the phrase, "space is the grace," highlights the value of creating a sense of spaciousness in our lives. When we give ourselves time and space to process our experiences, we are better able to respond in a way that is grounded and centered.

Finally, the third part of the phrase, "response is the power," underscores the importance of taking action based on our awareness and insights. By responding in a way that is thoughtful, compassionate, and aligned with our values, we can create positive change in our lives and in the world around us.

AND WHEN WE DO...

"Noticing is the Gift,
Space is the Grace,
Response is the Power"

WE CAN ACCEPT WHAT'S HERE NOW AND...

"DANCE WITH THE PARTNER YOU BROUGHT."

The phrase "dance with the partner you brought" is about embracing the present moment and making the most of what we have. By accepting the conditions of a situation, we can cultivate a sense of gratitude for the things we do have and find ways to work around the challenges we face.

This attitude of empowerment and resilience can help us to navigate even the most difficult of circumstances with grace and strength. In this space we can go inward rather than outward for the what we need to open up to our creativity and ability to move forward.

We will have many dances in our lives. When we are in a place that feels stuck or not within our control, we can pull in the phrase "dance with the partner you brought" and step into in a more empowered mind state even if it is a messy dance.

AND...

DANCE WITH THE PARTNER YOU BROUGHT

WE CAN REMEMBER...

"THINGS THAT MATTER TAKE EFFORT."

The understanding of "things that matter take effort" can be a difficult lesson to learn, as our minds are wired to seek pleasure and avoid pain. When something is challenging, our natural inclination is to give up or avoid it altogether.

However, it is important to remember that our muscles grow with a bit of tension. In the same way, our minds and abilities can grow when we acknowledge the hard work required and still move forward. When we understand the value that effort brings, we can empower ourselves to persist even in the face of challenges.

By acknowledging the hard work required and pushing through it, we can cultivate a sense of resilience and determination that will serve us well in all areas of our lives. Instead of avoiding that something is hard, we can see it as an opportunity to grow and become the best version of ourselves.

BUT...P.S. NOT EVERYTHING MATTERS...

Things that matter take effort

SOMETIMES WE WILL NEED TO...

"HOLD IT LIGHT."

The phrase "hold it light" is rooted in the idea that when we are feeling tight, angry, frustrated, and stuck, we should try to hold things with a lighter perspective. This means that instead of becoming consumed by negative thoughts and emotions, we should try to take a step back and look at the situation from a more objective viewpoint. By doing so, we can gain a greater sense of clarity and reduce the intensity of our emotions.

Holding things with a light perspective can be particularly useful in situations where we feel overwhelmed and out of control. Instead of focusing on the things that are causing us stress, we can try to shift our attention to the things that bring us joy and comfort. This can help to balance out the negative emotions and prevent us from becoming consumed by them.

Ultimately, the concept of "hold it light" is about finding a sense of balance and perspective in our lives. It is about recognizing that we cannot always control the things that happen to us, but we can control how we react to them. By holding things with a lighter perspective, we can reduce the impact of negative emotions and find a greater sense of peace and contentment in our lives.

EVEN THOUGH...

THAT CAN BE...

"EASY SAID HARD DO."

The phrase "easy said, hard do" is our reminder to be gentle with ourselves. It is not a free pass or way of giving up but a human way of acknowledging that what we might want or need to do could require a great deal of effort.

This phrase is often used to describe situations where people talk about their plans or goals without considering the actual work or effort required to achieve them. For example, saying that you'll start exercising every day may sound easy, but actually finding the time and motivation to do so can be difficult.

This phrase is also an opportunity to show compassion to others. We often give advice freely to those we care about, but we should instead offer compassion to someone who is stuck or struggling. Which is sometimes "easy said hard do".

WE HAVE TO REMEMBER...

EASY
SAID
HARD DO

OUR THOUGHTS AND EMOTIONS ARE...

"WHAT WE HAVE NOT WHAT WE ARE."

The phrase "what we have not what we are" pertains to the idea that our emotions and feelings are, not a part of our identity, but rather something we possess. This means that our emotions do not define us, but they are experiences that we go through. By separating our emotions from our identity, we can reduce the impact of negative emotions and avoid getting attached to them.

Often, we identify ourselves with our emotions, such as saying, "I am sad" or "I am angry," which can lead to a fixed mindset and resistance to change. By recognizing that emotions are something we experience, we can cultivate a growth mindset and become more resilient in dealing with them. This concept also emphasizes that our emotions are not permanent and change over time.

To apply this concept to our lives, we can practice mindfulness and observe our emotions without judgment or attachment. We can also cultivate self-awareness and identify the triggers that lead to certain emotions. By doing so, we can develop strategies to manage our emotions and prevent them from taking over our lives. Finally, we can focus on our actions rather than our emotions and work towards aligning our actions with our values and goals, even when we are experiencing negative emotions. By adopting this mindset, we can become more resilient, adaptable, and compassionate towards ourselves and others.

AND PERHAPS...

REST MIGHT BE WHAT IS NEEDED BECAUSE...

"WHAT YOU EMOTE YOU PROMOTE."

The phrase "what you emote you promote" refers to the idea that the emotions we express and convey to others can have an impact on how we are perceived and how we influence those around us. Essentially, when we display certain emotions, we are promoting those emotions and potentially encouraging others to feel the same way.

Social contagion is real. What we put out in the world is felt by others. When we are mindful, of this we can be intentional with what we emote. If we are in a difficult emotional place, we can have compassion for ourselves and allow rest. We can hold the understanding that thoughts and emotions are not permanent and time to rest can be just what is needed in the moment.

It's important to be aware of the emotions we are expressing and how they may be perceived by others. By consciously choosing to promote positive emotions and avoiding negative ones, we can create a more positive and productive environment for ourselves and those around us. Remember, what you emote, you promote.

FROM HERE...

WHAT YOU EMOTE YOU PROMOTE

WE CAN BEGIN TO....

"MAKE BIG SMALL."

The phrase "make big small" is all about breaking down big tasks or goals into smaller, more manageable pieces. This can be particularly useful when we feel overwhelmed by the day-to-day demands of life. When we are constantly bombarded with stimuli and responsibilities, it can be easy to become paralyzed by indecision and uncertainty. By making big things small, we can regain a sense of control and focus.

When we notice our minds becoming overwhelmed, it is important to acknowledge these feelings in the moment. Instead of ignoring or denying them, we can take a moment to pause and reflect on what is causing these feelings. By doing so, we can begin to identify the specific tasks or responsibilities that are contributing to our sense of overwhelm.

Once we have identified the specific tasks or responsibilities that are causing us stress, we can begin to break them down into smaller, more manageable pieces. By doing so, we can create a plan of action that feels more achievable and less daunting. This can help us to regain our focus and momentum, allowing us to move forward with purpose and intention.

AND...

MAKE
BIG
small

ALLOW CURIOSITY AND BE OPEN TO...

"PERHAPS, MAYBE, TOO SOON, DON'T KNOW."

The concept of "perhaps, maybe, too soon, don't know" is a powerful tool for keeping our minds open and avoiding the trap of certainty. When we become too sure of our own opinions or beliefs, we close ourselves off to new ideas and perspectives. By embracing the idea that we might not have all the answers, and that there is always more to learn, we can stay curious and open-minded, even in the face of uncertainty.

This mindset can be especially useful when we hear forecasts or predictions about the future. Rather than taking these predictions as gospel, we can approach them with a healthy dose of skepticism and a willingness to learn more.

By recognizing that we don't have all the information, and that there are often many factors that can influence future events, we can avoid getting too attached to any one outcome and remain open to new possibilities.

THEN WE CAN...

PERHAPS, MAYBE, TOO SOON,
DON'T KNOW

REFLECT ON OUR HABIT LOOPS AND DECIDE IT'S TIME TO...

"STOP CHEWING OLD GUM."

The concept of "stop chewing old gum" is a reminder that if we continue to do the same thing over and over again, we will continue to get the same results. This can be particularly relevant when it comes to negative thought patterns or behaviors that cause us frustration and suffering. Often, our minds build habit loops that can be difficult to break free from, even when the outcome is not desirable.

The key to breaking free from habit loops is to first recognize that they exist. When we notice ourselves getting stuck in a pattern of negative thoughts or behaviors, it is important to acknowledge this in the moment. By doing so, we can begin to take ownership of the pattern and work toward a different plan.

Once we have recognized the habit loop, we can begin to consciously break it by taking a different approach. This may mean challenging our thoughts or behaviors, or it may mean introducing new habits that are more positive and beneficial. Over time, with consistent effort, we can create new habit loops that better serve our needs and goals.

Ultimately, the concept of "stop chewing old gum" is a reminder that we have the power to change our habits and thought patterns. By recognizing when we are stuck in a negative loop and taking action to break free, we can cultivate a greater sense of agency and control over our lives. This can lead to greater happiness, fulfillment, and overall well-being.

AND MAYBE...

STOP
CHEWING
OLD GUM

PULL IN THE SILLY AND TRY NEW THINGS BECAUSE...

"HOKEY WORKS."

"Hokey works" is the concept of intentionally getting a little silly and uncomfortable to help us let go of our egos and take the seriousness out of things. When we engage in hokey works, we tap into our playful and childlike sides, which can help us to feel more creative, expansive, and open to new ideas. In essence, hokey works is a way of getting out of our own way so that we can connect more deeply with others and ourselves.

When we allow ourselves to be silly and playful, we open ourselves up to new possibilities and can often come up with more creative solutions to problems. Additionally, hokey works can help us to be more authentic and genuine in our interactions with others, as we're less concerned with maintaining a certain image or persona.

Another benefit of hokey works is that it can bring us closer to others. When we're willing to be a little silly and vulnerable, we create an atmosphere of trust and intimacy that can help to deepen our relationships. By letting our guards down and being willing to laugh at ourselves, we show others that we're not afraid to be imperfect and that we value their company and opinions. In this way, hokey works can be a powerful tool for building connections and fostering a sense of community.

WHILE REMEMBERING...

Honey Works

WHO WE SPEND THE MOST TIME WITH IS IMPORTANT AND ASK OURSELVES...

"WHO'S MY 5."

The phrase "who's my 5" refers to the idea that we are the average of the five people we spend the most time with. This means that the people we surround ourselves with can have a significant impact on our beliefs, behaviors, and overall sense of well-being.

This phrase highlights the importance of choosing our social circle carefully and being intentional about who we spend time with. It's important to surround ourselves with people who uplift and inspire us, challenge us to grow, and support us through the ups and downs of life.

Of course, it's not always possible to control who we interact with, especially in work or family situations. However, even in these circumstances, we can still strive to seek out positive influences and maintain healthy boundaries with those who may not have our best interests at heart.

In short, the phrase "who's my 5" emphasizes the importance of choosing our social circle carefully and being intentional about who we spend time with. By surrounding ourselves with positive, supportive individuals, we can cultivate a greater sense of well-being and fulfillment in our lives.

BUT ABOVE ALL...

WE MUST REMEMBER...

"DO NOT SEPARATE."

The phrase "do not separate is the reminder human beings are meant to come together. Despite our differences in culture, language, and beliefs, we all share basic human needs and experiences like the need for love, belonging, and understanding.

The phrase "do not separate" emphasizes the importance of recognizing our humanity and working towards unity rather than division. When we focus on our differences and separate ourselves from others, we literally put our mind and body in a state of tension and fear.

Instead, we should look up, see each other and build connections with others, even those who may seem different from us. By recognizing our common humanity, we can create a sense of compassion and empathy that promotes understanding and acceptance.

In today's world, it's more important than ever to remember our commonality and just see each other. Indifference is one of the most dangerous states of mind for any human to have. "Do not separate" is a powerful reminder to watch for our indifference and to cultivate one of the most healthy mind states, that of common humanity.

WE ARE ALWAYS BETTER TOGETHER...

DO NOT
SEPARATE

AND FROM HERE WE CAN BEGIN TO SET OUR...

INTENTION

Now that you have read the book, take a moment to reflect on what you learned and how it can benefit you in your personal and professional life. Think about the key takeaways and insights you gained from the book and how you can apply them to your daily life.

Remember, knowledge is only powerful when it is put into action. So, take the first step towards applying the concepts by setting clear and achievable goals for yourself. Create a plan of action and make a commitment to follow through with it.

It's important to keep in mind that change and growth take time, effort, and persistence. Don't get discouraged if progress feels slow at first. Every step you take towards applying the concepts from the book is a step in the right direction.

Finally, believe in yourself and your ability to make positive changes in your life. With dedication and perseverance, you can achieve your goals and create a better life for yourself. Good luck on your journey!

BECAUSE THE BEST WAY IS JUST TO START...

the best way is just to start!

INTENTACT
Intentions to Actions Leadership

This quote highlights the three important aspects that are necessary for any journey of personal growth and development.

First, the quote mentions the "whisper of wisdom," which implies that the journey starts with a small seed of knowledge or insight. It could be something that is learned from a mentor or a book, or perhaps a realization that comes from personal experience. Whatever the source, this initial insight serves as the starting point for the journey of growth and change.

Next, the quote emphasizes the importance of science, suggesting that knowledge and wisdom must be supported by evidence-based research and practical application. This means that the journey of growth and development cannot rely solely on intuition or subjective experiences, but must also be grounded in objective knowledge and proven methods.

Finally, the quote mentions the importance of living in the practice of life, which emphasizes the need for consistent effort and application of knowledge and skills. Personal growth is not a one-time event, but rather an ongoing process that requires discipline and dedication. It is through consistent practice that new habits are formed, and old patterns are broken.

By starting with a small seed of wisdom, supporting it with science, and living in the practice of life, individuals can embark on a journey of growth and transformation that leads to a more fulfilling and purposeful life.

WANT MORE...

"The journey begins with the whisper of wisdom, supported by the science, and lived in the practice of life"

WANT MORE

At IntentAct, we are dedicated to helping individuals and corporations achieve their full potential through our comprehensive range of services. Our services include personal coaching, self-help guided meditations, and exclusive programs like MPEAK and IntentAct X.

We pride ourselves on our commitment to excellence and our ability to deliver results that make a real difference. Whether you're looking for personal growth or organizational success, we are here to support you every step of the way.

Visit our website at www.intentat.com to learn more about how IntentAct can help you unlock your full potential and achieve your goals.

Whether you're looking for inspiration, guidance, or simply a beautiful book to enjoy, this collection of quotes and mantras is sure to leave a lasting impact.

PERSONAL COACHING
MINDFUL ONE ON ONE

CORPORATE WORKSHOPS
MINDFUL WORKPLACE WORKSHOPS

mPEAK
Mindfulness Meditation + Sports & Positive Psychology + Neuroscience + Group Coaching = mPEAK

INTENTACT X
8 WEEK MINDFULNESS COURSE

MINDFUL RETREATS
MINDFUL GETAWAY

GUIDED MEDITATION
RECORDED MEDITATIONS

Pam is the principle owner of Intentions to Actions Leadership. A Mindfulness based leadership company that centers around helping individuals and organizations identify their desired leadership intentions in both personal and professional life. With the structure of utilizing traditional leadership development model combined with the foundations of mindfulness Pam helps to guide a roadmap with actions that align to those intentions.

Pam came to mindful leadership coaching after spending 25 plus years as a senior corporate executive with various large fortune 500 companies. During her final years in her previous career path Pam began her own personal journey of mindfulness. In 2019 Pam became a fully certified instructor of mPEAK (Mindful, Performance, Enhancement and Knowledge) through University of Southern California.

When not helping others through work or volunteering Pam enjoys being in nature and spending time with family and friends.

Pam while progressing in her career, moving throughout the country always had her greatest source of pride with her, her son Casey. Raising Casey alone but always supported by family and deep personal friends Pam gives gratitude reflection daily for the gifts of those she has in her life.

Everything begins with awareness...
NOTICING IS THE GIFT, SPACE IS THE GRACE, RESPONSE IS THE POWER
and when we do...

we can accept what's here now and...
DANCE WITH THE PARTNER WE BROUGHT
and...

we can remember...
THINGS THAT MATTER TAKE EFFORT
but P.S. not everything matters...

sometimes we will need to...
HOLD IT LIGHT
even though ...

that can be...
EASY SAID HARD DO
we have to remember...

our thoughts and emotions are...
WHAT WE HAVE, NOT WHAT WE ARE
and perhaps...

rest might be what is needed because...
WHAT WE EMOTE, WE PROMOTE
and from here...

we can begin to...
MAKE BIG SMALL
and...

allow curiosity and be open to...
PERHAPS MAYBE TOO SOON DON'T KNOW
we can...

reflect on our habit loops and decide it's time to...
STOP CHEWING OLD GUM
and ...

pull in the silly and try new things because, well...
HOKEY WORKS
while remembering...

who we spend the most time with is important and ask ourselves...
WHO'S MY FIVE
but above all...

we must remember...
DO NOT SEPARATE
we are always better together...

and from here we can begin to...
SET OUR INTENTIONS
because the best way is just to start...

THE JOURNEY BEGINS WITH A WHISPER OF WISDOM,
SUPPORTED BY THE SCIENCE, AND
LIVED IN THE PRACTICE OF LIFE.

"Noticing is the Gift, Space is the Grace, Response is the Power"

DANCE WITH THE PARTNER YOU BROUGHT

Things that matter Take Effort

Hold it Light

EASY SAID HARD DO

WHAT WE HAVE NOT WHAT WE ARE

WHAT YOU EMOTE YOU PROMOTE

MAKE BIG small

PERHAPS MAYBE, TOO SOON
DON'T KNOW

STOP
CHEWING
OLD GUM

BIG TEXAN

honey works

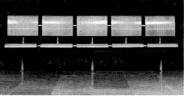

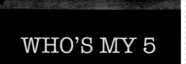

WHO'S MY 5

DO NOT
separate

the best way is just to start!

"The journey begins with the whisper of wisdom, supported by the science, and lived in the practice of life"

IN YOUR OWN WORDS

_____

Made in the USA
Monee, IL
19 August 2023

41285426R00026